Microsoft
Power Apps

The Microsoft 365 Companion Series

Dr. Patrick Jones

OLYMPUS ACADEMY
PRESS

TABLE OF CONTENTS

EMPOWERING INNOVATION WITH POWER APPS

In a world where workplaces run on endless spreadsheets, email attachments, and manual processes, achieving streamlined efficiency can feel like an uphill battle. Many organizations rely on custom software for critical needs—yet developing in-house apps often requires specialized coding knowledge, large budgets, or lengthy timelines. Microsoft Power Apps offers a more accessible path: a platform that lets you (yes, even if you're not a professional developer) build custom apps to solve problems and unify data without writing endless lines of code.

Picture being able to drag and drop elements onto a canvas, connecting them to SharePoint lists, Excel files, or other data sources in a matter of clicks. Now imagine handing that app to your coworkers on their phones or in Microsoft Teams so they can track inventory, submit approvals, or update records in real time. That's the promise of Power Apps—a tool designed to empower everyone to innovate.

Microsoft Power Apps is part of the Power Platform, alongside Power Automate, Power BI, and Power Virtual Agents. Each tool addresses a different challenge—automation, analytics, and chatbots—yet they all share a foundation of user-friendly design and deep Microsoft 365 integration. For Power Apps specifically, the goal is to give you the freedom to build applications that capture data, kick off approvals, or update records, all with minimal coding.

It's an ideal fit for teams looking to reduce repetitive tasks (like emailing forms back and forth), create mobile-friendly tools for fieldwork, or unify existing data sources under one intuitive interface. You don't need to be a developer to harness this power. If you can create flowcharts in

Visio or shapes in PowerPoint, you're already thinking in the visual terms that Power Apps uses.

If you've followed our other Microsoft 365 companion books, you know Sarah well. She's a busy team leader who's already streamlined processes with Power Automate and adopted data-driven insights with Power BI. Yet she keeps encountering a gap: her colleagues need simple apps to track project tasks, submit requests, or update their inventory on the go, and the IT team's backlog for custom solutions stretches on for months.

- **Problem**: Sarah's team currently logs tasks in Excel sheets scattered across OneDrive folders. Finding updated versions or collecting new data is a nightmare.

- **Discovery**: A coworker mentioned Power Apps as a quick way to transform a spreadsheet into a mobile-friendly data-entry interface.

- **Goal**: Empower the team to build a self-service app that standardizes data collection, supports real-time collaboration, and cuts down on repetitive emails.

Intrigued, Sarah starts exploring Power Apps. She's not a coder, but as she opens the design canvas and sees a tool that looks like Microsoft's other drag-and-drop platforms, she realizes the learning curve might be easier than she thought.

The best part about Power Apps? It's not just for software developers. Anyone comfortable with logic-based thinking or with a desire to automate processes can build basic (and even moderately advanced) apps:

- Project Managers needing a quick way to track tasks and deadlines

- HR Teams looking for an internal portal to submit leave requests or onboard employees

- Sales Reps requiring mobile-friendly tools to update client visits in real time

- Administrators wanting a centralized database for inventory, equipment requests, or approvals

From small businesses to global enterprises, if you have a process that's bogged down by manual steps or scattered across multiple spreadsheets, Power Apps can be a game-changer.

We'll guide you from basic app design to advanced integrations, showing how to tie Power Apps into your Microsoft 365 ecosystem—like embedding apps in Teams or linking them to SharePoint lists. Expect plenty of practical tips, real-life examples, and pointers on avoiding pitfalls along the way.

1. **Introduction**
   - Gain a broad view of what Power Apps is and why it's revolutionizing low-code development.

2. **What Is Power Apps?**
   - Dive deeper into the platform's components, core features, and how it fits into the Power Platform.

3. **Why Use Power Apps?**
   - Explore the advantages of building apps in-house, from faster iteration cycles to cost savings.

4. **Get Started**
   - Get hands-on with your first app: learning the interface, data connections, and basic form creation.

5. **Best Practices**
   - Discover how to design user-friendly screens, handle data validations, and structure your app for long-term maintenance.

6. **Tips and Tricks**

- o Level up with advanced concepts like conditional formatting, environment variables, offline capabilities, and responsive design.

7. **Copilot**

- o See how AI-driven suggestions can help you build screens or design logic flows faster, even if you're new to Power Apps.

8. **Common Pitfalls**

- o Learn how to avoid typical snags—like performance issues or overcomplicated formulas—that can derail even the best intentions.

9. **Episode About Sarah**

- o Follow Sarah's personal journey, from creating her first app to inspiring a wave of citizen development across her organization.

10. **Summary and Reflection**

- o Recap the book's key lessons, ensuring you're ready to keep evolving in the Power Apps universe.

11. **Final Thoughts**

- o Reflect on how Power Apps fits into the broader Microsoft 365 ecosystem and discover resources for continuous growth.

By the end of this book, you'll understand how to bring data, logic, and user interfaces together in ways that simplify workflows and solve real business problems. Like Sarah, you might be surprised at how quickly you can stand up a functional app—no coding bootcamp required.

Ready to transform those messy spreadsheets and endless email chains into sleek, mobile-friendly tools that your colleagues will actually enjoy using? Let's begin by unpacking What Is Power Apps?—your gateway to unlocking a new era of innovation within Microsoft 365. Grab your data ideas, bring your enthusiasm, and let's harness the power of low-code to build apps that make a real difference!

WHAT IS POWER APPS?

Think of an app you can build in minutes—without extensive coding—that unifies data, streamlines tasks, and can be used on any device. That's Microsoft Power Apps. Part of Microsoft's Power Platform (which also includes Power Automate, Power BI, and Power Virtual Agents), Power Apps is designed to bring low-code development to everyone, enabling you to craft custom applications for everyday business challenges. From simple forms that replace paper-based processes to more intricate solutions that integrate with multiple data sources, Power Apps hands you the toolkit to build tailor-made apps—fast.

Traditionally, building business applications was a job for professional developers or IT departments, requiring specialized programming languages. Power Apps changes that paradigm by offering a visual, drag-and-drop approach. Whether you're a project manager, an HR specialist, or an admin with basic tech know-how, Power Apps helps you transform ideas into functional apps that run on desktops, tablets, and smartphones.

Core Components of Power Apps

1. **Canvas Apps**

   o A blank canvas where you drag and drop controls—like text fields, buttons, or drop-downs—and connect them to data sources. Perfect if you want full control over your layout and user interface.

2. **Model-Driven Apps**

   o Built on Microsoft Dataverse (the Power Platform's underlying data service). Instead of designing each screen from scratch, you define data models and business processes. Power Apps then auto-generates a user-friendly interface.

3. **Portals**

    o   Create external-facing websites that interact with your
        data. Great for allowing customers or partners to log in
        and submit forms, track service tickets, or view account
        details.

No matter your choice—canvas, model-driven, or portals—you can
integrate with hundreds of data sources, from SharePoint lists to on-
premises databases, all secured under the Microsoft 365 umbrella.

If you've followed our companion books, you know Sarah as the
resourceful team lead who's embraced tools like Power Automate for
automation and Power BI for analytics. Despite these advancements, she
still faced issues collecting data from her colleagues, who struggled with
multiple Excel sheets and email attachments. Creating a custom
application through traditional software development seemed
daunting—and outside the scope of IT's busy schedule.

Enter Power Apps. With a few clicks, Sarah discovered she could link
her SharePoint lists into a sleek interface, letting her team submit project
updates on their phones. No more version-control nightmares, and no
more manually merging everyone's spreadsheets. That initial success
sparked her curiosity: what else could she build?

Nearly anyone in an organization can benefit, from individual "citizen
developers" to IT professionals:

*   **Citizen Developers**: Non-IT staff who see a process gap—like
    inconsistent data entry or clunky approvals—and want to fix it
    themselves.

*   **IT and Pro Developers**: For advanced scenarios, Power Apps
    integrates with custom code, Azure services, and more. It speeds
    up development while still allowing for deep customization.

*   **Business Analysts**: Those who combine domain knowledge
    with basic logical thinking can rapidly prototype new solutions,
    then refine them through user feedback.

- **Managers and Leaders**: People needing quick solutions for everyday tasks—employee onboardings, inventory checks, or simple data-collection forms—without waiting months for an official app rollout.

In short, if you have a repetitive or error-prone process, or you rely on multiple disjointed data sources, Power Apps can help unify and simplify how information flows across your team.

At a high level, Power Apps blends three core elements:

1. **Data Sources**

   o Connect to SharePoint lists, Excel files, SQL databases, Dynamics 365, or external services like Salesforce. Use Microsoft Dataverse if you need a robust, scalable backend to store and manage data.

2. **Logic and Expressions**

   o Like Excel formulas, Power Apps expressions let you control behavior—what happens when a user taps a button or changes a dropdown. You can filter records, update fields, and call external APIs with familiar, formula-like syntax.

3. **User Interface**

   o Create screens (pages) that hold text inputs, galleries (lists), forms, and other controls. In Canvas Apps, you design the layout freely, placing controls anywhere. Model-driven apps derive layouts from your data model, saving you design time.

The result is an app that feels modern and intuitive, which you can share via Microsoft Teams, the Power Apps mobile app, or embed in a website.

Power Apps isn't isolated. It works seamlessly with:

- Power Automate to automate workflows triggered by app actions

- Power BI to embed dashboards inside your app or see data from your app in analytics
- Power Virtual Agents to chat with your data or run advanced AI-based tasks

This synergy means that once your app is up and running, you can extend its functionality:

- A button in Power Apps could trigger a Power Automate flow.
- Visuals from Power BI can provide real-time insights within your app.
- Chatbots from Power Virtual Agents might answer user questions or guide them through the app's steps.

Sarah's Discovery: She added a "Submit" button in her project-tracking app that instantly triggered a Power Automate flow, sending an email to her manager if any updates flagged high-risk issues. One small integration saved her from manually checking for urgent tasks.

Power Apps aims to lower the technical barrier. If you can design a PowerPoint slide or write an Excel formula, you have the foundation to build a simple canvas app. The software's guided approach, coupled with built-in templates, means you won't be starting from scratch. Add some practice (and maybe some help from AI-driven Copilot), and you'll be customizing forms, dropdowns, and logic in no time.

Sarah's First App: She picked a SharePoint list containing project updates and used the Canvas App template to generate a basic interface. Power Apps automatically created a browse screen, detail screen, and edit screen. Sarah customized it to match her team's branding and added a quick "Notify Manager" button. Once shared, her team used it from their phones within a day—no lengthy dev cycle needed.

GROWING WITH YOUR NEEDS

- **Scalable Data**: Start small with Excel or SharePoint; later, move to Dataverse if you need more robust relational structures or advanced security.

- **Complex Logic**: If out-of-the-box formulas aren't enough, developers can extend functionality with Power Fx or integrate Azure services.

- **Custom Connectors**: Connect to 3rd-party APIs or unique line-of-business systems if you require data beyond built-in connectors.

You can remain a "citizen developer," or push the platform's limits with professional dev skills. Power Apps doesn't lock you into a single skill level; it grows as you do.

At its core, Microsoft Power Apps is about giving everyone a chance to solve problems. Where you once had to rely on IT or developers for every custom solution, you can now design functional apps yourself—turning ad-hoc spreadsheets and manual processes into modern apps. Whether you're a small business owner wanting an easy inventory tracker, a sales rep who needs on-the-go updates, or a large enterprise bridging multiple data systems, Power Apps can be your launchpad for continuous innovation.

In our next chapter, we'll explore why you might use Power Apps over traditional development or other low-code platforms. From cost savings to faster iteration cycles, you'll see how easy it is to convert day-to-day challenges into solutions your entire team can use. Like Sarah, you may be surprised at just how quickly you can transform ideas into fully functioning apps—no coding background required!

WHY USE POWER APPS?

In a landscape where everyday business challenges often require nimble, custom solutions, Microsoft Power Apps stands out by making app creation accessible to non-developers. Imagine having the ability to build a functional mobile or web app that perfectly matches your team's needs—without waiting months for IT resources or learning a complex programming language. Whether you're an office administrator automating paper-based forms or a manager needing a fast way to record field data, Power Apps provides a shortcut to innovation. But why invest time in learning yet another tool? In this chapter, we'll break down the benefits of Power Apps, focusing on its low-code design, rich integration with Microsoft 365, and capacity to empower everyday users—like Sarah—to bring transformative ideas to life.

1. A TRUE LOW-CODE EXPERIENCE

Traditional app development requires knowledge of languages like C#, Java, or Swift. Power Apps, however, introduces an environment where app-building feels more like configuring Excel formulas and PowerPoint slides. You drag and drop controls onto a canvas, link them to data sources, and define behaviors with a formula bar reminiscent of Excel. This approach lets you focus on logic and usability rather than wrestling with syntax.

Prototyping is crucial in modern workplaces where feedback loops must be short. Because Power Apps is low-code, you can mock up a functional prototype in a single afternoon, show it to your team, get feedback, and iterate. The gap between idea and tangible app shrinks, encouraging creative experimentation that might never happen if you had to wait for a full-scale development project.

Sarah's Early Win
When Sarah wanted a quick app for tracking team tasks, she picked a

Power Apps Canvas App template. Within an hour, she had a basic form for people to submit updates. That near-instant prototype validated the concept—had she waited for IT to code a solution, the idea might have languished in her email drafts.

2. SEAMLESS MICROSOFT 365 INTEGRATION

Microsoft Power Apps sits natively within the Power Platform but integrates deeply with Microsoft 365. If your data resides in SharePoint, Excel, or OneDrive, you can link it to Power Apps with minimal setup. Need to embed your app in a Teams channel? That's a few clicks. The result: you don't have to switch services or pay for extra connectors just to unify your workflow.

Because Power Apps leverages your existing Azure Active Directory identity, you don't need separate logins or complicated permission schemes. Row-level security can be enforced through your existing Microsoft 365 groups, ensuring that each user only sees data they're allowed to see. This synergy also means your app adheres to organizational compliance, data loss prevention policies, and encryption standards by default.

Sarah's Synergy
Sarah's organization already used SharePoint to store project details. Power Apps recognized her Microsoft 365 credentials, fetched the relevant lists, and let her build forms that read and wrote data in real time. She didn't have to define new user logins or create complicated security rules—Microsoft 365 handled it behind the scenes.

3. CONNECTORS TO VAST DATA SOURCES

Beyond Microsoft 365, Power Apps can tap into hundreds of connectors, from popular SaaS tools (Salesforce, Dropbox) to on-premises databases via a gateway. Each connector abstracts away complex authentication or API calls. You simply pick the service, sign in, and select the tables or endpoints you need.

If you have a unique line-of-business app or a proprietary API, you can build custom connectors. Once created, it works like any built-in connector, letting you surface specialized data or trigger actions within Power Apps. This approach merges low-code convenience with the flexibility to integrate your own systems.

Sarah's Data Integration
As her app evolved, Sarah added a connector for her organization's CRM (an external system). Power Apps then pulled customer IDs and statuses directly into the same interface the team used for project tasks, unifying everything in a single place. Her manager was thrilled—less toggling between systems meant less confusion and fewer data mismatches.

4. EMPOWERING CITIZEN DEVELOPERS AND IT COLLABORATION

Power Apps democratizes app creation. Historically, building software was reserved for professional developers. Now, citizen developers—the frontline employees who understand the real operational gaps—can craft solutions themselves. They know the workflows, pain points, and best shortcuts. With Power Apps, they solve their own problems, often more effectively than an external dev who lacks that insight.

This doesn't mean IT is sidelined. In fact, IT can oversee the process, ensuring apps meet security and compliance standards. Pro developers can step in to extend apps with Azure services or custom code, bridging advanced features. The result is a hybrid approach: citizen developers handle day-to-day solutions, while IT sets guardrails and handles deep customizations.

Sarah's IT Partnership
While Sarah created most of her project-tracking app using low-code features, she teamed up with IT for a specialized approval step requiring an Azure-based identity check. IT wrote a small piece of code, integrated

it through a custom connector, and the entire process remained aligned with corporate security policies.

5. MOBILE-FRIENDLY DESIGN OUT OF THE BOX

A huge advantage of Power Apps is mobile-first design. When you create a Canvas App, you can choose a phone or tablet layout. The drag-and-drop canvas then generates a responsive interface with tap-friendly controls. Users can run the finished app through the Power Apps mobile app on iOS or Android, with no extra deployment steps.

For scenarios where the network is spotty (like field inspections or warehouse checkouts), you can enable offline capabilities. Data is temporarily stored on the device and synced back to the source once the connection resumes. This fosters productivity in remote or on-the-go situations that typically hamper web-based forms.

Sarah's Field Advantage

Her team occasionally worked offsite, auditing construction sites where Wi-Fi was unreliable. By configuring her Power Apps solution for offline mode, staff could capture photos, notes, and checklists on their phones, then sync automatically when they returned to an internet-connected environment.

6. RAPID ITERATION AND COST SAVINGS

With minimal code to write, you skip the typical dev cycle of writing, debugging, and compiling. Power Apps visually indicates how each control or expression behaves, letting you spot errors quickly. Need a new field? Drag in a text input, bind it to your data, and go—no manual database scripts or complicated migrations.

Traditional app projects can be expensive, both in upfront dev costs and ongoing maintenance. Power Apps often cuts that cost dramatically, especially for internal tools that don't require high-level enterprise features. The time saved from not coding or manually merging data equates to real dollars.

Sarah's Efficiency Gains

She remembers an old custom-built tool that took months to develop and needed frequent IT patches. By contrast, her new Power Apps project launched in weeks and was mostly maintained by the business team itself. No large developer fees, no lengthy approval cycles—just agile iteration.

7. EASY UPDATES AND SHARING

When you update a Power Apps solution, changes appear automatically for all users. There's no need to redistribute an install package or have everyone download an updated app binary. In the Power Apps Service, you simply publish the latest version, and the next time your users open the app, they see the improvements.

Need feedback from a coworker? Add them as a co-owner of the app. They can open the Power Apps editor, make changes, and test them right alongside you. For large-scale rollouts, you can embed the app in Teams channels or SharePoint pages so the entire group knows where to find it.

Sarah's Cooperative Work

After building the core features, Sarah gave her colleague access to the editor to refine some UI elements. Together, they tested new color themes and rearranged certain fields for better flow. The next morning, they published it to the entire marketing department—no separate deployment or update instructions required.

8. INTEGRATING AI WITH COPILOT

One of the newest additions to Power Apps is Copilot, an AI-driven assistant that helps with building screens, connecting data, or even generating formulas. Instead of scouring documentation, you can ask

Copilot in plain English, "Create a gallery that displays my top 10 leads sorted by revenue," and watch it generate the UI and logic.

Copilot can also guide you through issues—like "Why doesn't this dropdown show the correct items?"—and propose solutions in real time, speeding up your troubleshooting. It's like having a friendly coding mentor sitting next to you 24/7.

Sarah's AI Boost

Sarah discovered she could type "Copilot, add a screen that pulls manager approvals from my SharePoint list," and Copilot would scaffold a new screen with fields and a patch formula. Instead of fumbling with expressions, she tweaked the generated code to match her naming conventions, cutting hours off her dev time.

9. A LAUNCHPAD FOR BUSINESS TRANSFORMATION

Power Apps excels at handling small departmental apps—like a budget tracker or an event registration form. As you gain confidence, you can expand into model-driven apps, integrate with enterprise data, or build robust portals for external users. There's no cap on how advanced you can go.

Perhaps the biggest reason to use Power Apps is the culture change it fosters. Encouraging staff to become problem-solvers rather than passive users unleashes new ideas, speeds up digital transformation, and reduces reliance on shadow IT solutions. When employees can shape their own apps, they feel more ownership and pride in their workflows.

Sarah's Vision

Seeing how her first app significantly reduced email clutter, she encouraged each department to identify one process to transform with Power Apps. Soon, HR launched a "Leave Request" form, and Finance introduced a "CapEx Request" app. The entire company shifted from "We can't do that, we lack resources" to "Let's see if Power Apps can handle it!"

Why use Power Apps? Because it empowers every level of your organization to innovate, bridging gaps traditionally reliant on specialized coding. It aligns perfectly with Microsoft 365 data, extends to a multitude of connectors, and scales from quick prototypes to sophisticated enterprise solutions. And with the addition of AI features like Copilot, building and refining your app has never been more user-friendly.

Up next, we'll move from the "why" to the "how." In the following chapters, we'll explore the steps to get started with Power Apps—covering interface basics, data connections, and the creation of your very first app. Like Sarah, you'll see how a small leap into low-code can yield rapid, meaningful improvements in your day-to-day operations. Let's begin!

GETTING STARTED WITH MICROSOFT POWER APPS

You've explored what Power Apps is and why it can make a difference. Now, it's time for the how. In this chapter, we'll guide you through the initial steps of installing Power Apps, choosing the right app type, and creating your first simple solution. Whether you're looking to replace a paper form, streamline data entry, or build a small mobile tool, this is where the magic begins. Sarah, our Microsoft 365 champion, also started from these basics—learning the interface, connecting data, and gradually discovering how easy it is to bring an idea to life.

1. CHOOSING YOUR APP TYPE: CANVAS, MODEL-DRIVEN, OR PORTALS

Before diving in, decide which type of Power App suits your scenario:

1. **Canvas Apps**

   o A blank canvas where you design every screen, place controls (buttons, text fields, galleries) wherever you like, and connect to various data sources. This is great if you want full creative control over the layout.

2. **Model-Driven Apps**

   o Centered on your Dataverse data model. Power Apps auto-generates much of the interface—forms, views, and dashboards—based on your entity definitions. Best for apps that revolve around structured processes, like a case management or customer service scenario.

3. **Portals**

   o Create public or partner-facing websites that tie into Dataverse data and logic. Perfect if you want external users (e.g., customers) to log in, submit requests, or view account info without needing an internal Microsoft 365 account.

Sarah's First Choice:
She opted for a Canvas App to create a custom layout for her team's project-tracking needs. She liked the freedom to design the screen flow and rearrange controls to match how her colleagues typically worked.

2. ACCESSING POWER APPS

In the Microsoft 365 Portal

1. Go to office.com and Sign In

    o   Use your Microsoft 365 credentials.

2. Select "Power Apps"

    o   Sometimes found under "All apps" if not pinned.

3. Access the Power Apps Home

    o   Here, you'll see various options: "Start from template," "Dataverse," or "Blank app."

Alternatively, navigate to make.powerapps.com, which takes you straight to the Power Apps maker portal. You'll see your environment selector in the top-right corner (if you have multiple environments).

Sarah's Setup:
She went to make.powerapps.com, signed in with her work credentials, and landed on the maker portal. On the left-hand menu, she noticed tabs for Apps, Data, Flows, and Chatbots (the latter for Power Virtual Agents). This unified interface gave her a quick sense of the entire Power Platform.

3. SELECTING A DATA SOURCE

Before creating your app, think: where does your data live?

- **SharePoint List**: Ideal for quick use-cases; easy to link.

- **Excel**: Basic scenarios if your data is in OneDrive or SharePoint.

- **Dataverse**: For robust relational data, better security, and advanced features.

- **SQL, Dynamics 365, or Third-Party**: Use built-in or custom connectors.

Sarah's Data:

Her team's tasks resided in a SharePoint list called "ProjectTasks." Each item had columns for Title, AssignedTo, DueDate, Status, and Notes. She decided to build a Power App around that list so colleagues could add and update tasks from their phones.

4. CREATING YOUR FIRST CANVAS APP

Step 1: Click "Create App"

1. From the Maker Portal, choose Create in the left navigation.

2. Select "Canvas app from blank" (or pick a data-driven template if you want a head start).

3. Name Your App and pick "Phone" or "Tablet" layout. If you plan mobile use, choose "Phone."

Step 2: Connect to Data

1. Open the Data Pane on the left side.

2. Add Data > choose your connector (e.g., SharePoint).

3. Authenticate and select the list or table you want (Sarah picked her "ProjectTasks" list).

Step 3: Add Screens and Controls

1. By default, you start with a blank Screen1.

2. **Insert a Gallery**: In the top ribbon, select Insert → Gallery → pick a layout (e.g., Vertical).

3. **Bind It to Your Data**: Under the Items property, set it to your data source (e.g., "ProjectTasks").

   o Instantly, you'll see a scrollable list of tasks.

4. **Customize Fields**: In the right panel, choose which fields appear—like Title, DueDate, and Status.

Sarah's First Screen:
She inserted a vertical gallery, saw placeholders labeled "ThisItem.Title," "ThisItem.AssignedTo," etc., and realized how quickly the app was pulling from her SharePoint columns. Editing the text formatting and color was as simple as clicking properties and changing values—like she would in PowerPoint.

5. ADDING A FORM TO CREATE OR EDIT RECORDS

Step 1: Insert an Edit Form

1. Go to Insert → Forms → Edit Form.

2. Place It on your screen (maybe a second screen for clarity, so Screen2 is your "Detail/Edit" screen).

Step 2: Bind It to Your Data

1. Select the form, set Data Source = "ProjectTasks."

2. Fields: Choose which columns to include. The form auto-creates input fields.

Step 3: Submission Logic

1. Add a Button (Insert → Button) labeled "Save."

2. OnSelect Property: Use SubmitForm(EditForm1).

3. Navigation: After submission, you might want to go back to Screen1 with Navigate(Screen1, None).

Sarah's Setup:
She created a "Task Details" screen with an edit form bound to

"ProjectTasks." Tapping a record in the gallery on Screen1 navigated to Screen2, where her team could update status or add notes. The "Save" button used SubmitForm(EditForm1) then returned them to the gallery screen. Within minutes, she had a simple CRUD (Create, Read, Update, Delete) flow.

6. POLISHING THE APP

Layout and Theme

- **Rearrange Controls**: Drag text fields where you want them.

- **Insert Icons**: Buttons aren't the only clickable elements; icons (like a pencil or trash can) can be more intuitive for "edit" or "delete."

- **Use Themes**: In the Home tab, pick a theme for color consistency.

Basic Validation

- **Required Fields**: Mark them in your data source or form field settings.

- **Conditional Visibility**: If a user picks "Completed" as status, you could hide "DueDate" with an expression like Visible = Status <> "Completed".

Testing

- **Preview Mode**: Click the Play icon in the top-right corner to test your app.

- **Test Each Screen**: Add a new record, edit an existing one, navigate around. Make sure everything flows logically.

Sarah's Aha Moment:
Adding a bright "+" icon in the top corner of the main gallery let her open a blank form to create a new task. She then discovered a built-in

"Trash" icon she used for the remove action. The app started to look and feel like a real production tool, not just a quick mockup.

7. SHARING YOUR APP

Publishing and Sharing

1. **Save and Publish**: In the upper right, pick File → Save. Then choose Publish in the Power Apps maker portal to finalize changes.

2. **Manage Roles**: If you're the creator, you can add co-owners or just share with specific people or groups.

3. **User Access**: Recipients see the app under "My Apps" in the **Power Apps** portal or mobile app.

Embedding in Teams or SharePoint

- **Teams**: Add a Power Apps tab in a channel, select your app.

- **SharePoint**: Insert a web part for Power Apps, paste the app's web link.

Sarah's Rollout:
She shared her "ProjectTasks" app with her marketing team's security group. Each colleague simply opened the Power Apps mobile app, found "ProjectTasks" in "Shared with me," and tapped to launch. Some pinned it in their phone's home screen for easy access on-the-go.

8. ITERATE AND GROW

1. **Gather Feedback**: Ask your team: "What else do we need? Are any columns missing? Should we add a filter or different view?"

2. **Add More Features**: Perhaps a second screen for advanced reporting or a Copilot-driven question pane that helps users find tasks by phrase.

3. **Leverage Copilot**: If available, type queries like "Copilot, create a quick scoreboard for due tasks," and see if it can help generate relevant components.

Sarah's Continuous Improvement:
Her colleagues asked for a quick overview of "tasks due this week." She created a filter button that used Filter(ProjectTasks, DueDate <= Today() + 7, Status <> "Completed"), updating the main gallery to show upcoming tasks. Feedback was immediate: "This is so helpful!" She iterated again, letting users sort by priority or assigned user.

You've now built your first Power App—an interactive, data-driven tool that your team can use on any device. From here, the doors open to endless possibilities:

- **Advanced Use**: Explore model-driven apps if you need structured processes or a built-in sitemap.

- **Dataverse**: If your data calls for deeper relationships and security, consider migrating from SharePoint or Excel to Microsoft Dataverse.

- **Integrations**: Connect your app to Power Automate for automated workflows, or embed Power BI visuals to show real-time analytics in-app.

- **AI with Copilot**: For generating screens, forms, or logic flows more quickly, rely on Copilot's suggestions as you expand your app's capabilities.

Like Sarah, you may be surprised by how quickly a simple form can evolve into a robust enterprise tool that solves real, day-to-day problems. The best part? You, the citizen developer, are now at the helm, steering app development without needing a full dev team.

In the next chapters, we'll explore best practices for designing user-friendly Power Apps, deeper tips and tricks, and how to harness Copilot.

Step by step, you'll refine your new skills and discover that no process is too small or too big for the world of low-code.

BEST PRACTICES FOR MICROSOFT POWER APPS

Building your first app in Power Apps can be exhilarating—especially when you realize how quickly you can convert manual processes into sleek, mobile-friendly solutions. But once you go beyond the basics, certain principles emerge that can keep your app robust, user-friendly, and scalable. In this chapter, we'll explore the best practices that help you avoid confusion, maintain consistency, and ensure your Power App stands the test of time. You'll see how Sarah, our ever-resourceful project lead, refined her own approach to tackle everything from naming conventions to data security.

1. START WITH A CLEAR DATA STRUCTURE

Why It Matters

Your app's success often hinges on how well you organize and link your data sources. A messy SharePoint list or inconsistent Excel columns can lead to complicated patches, forms that break, or confusing user experiences.

Best Practices

1. **Define Data First**

   o Decide where your data lives (e.g., SharePoint, Excel, Dataverse). Set up tables with clear, consistent column names before building screens.

2. **Use Logical Field Names**

   o Rename "Column1" to something descriptive like "TaskStatus." This clarity prevents guesswork later on.

3. **Normalize Where Possible**

- For bigger apps, consider separating data into multiple lists or tables if you have repeating sets (e.g., a lookup table for statuses).

Sarah's Example

When Sarah kicked off her "ProjectTasks" app, she first reorganized the SharePoint list columns. She replaced cryptic column headers with user-friendly names ("TaskTitle," "DueDate") so that forms made sense instantly.

2. ADOPT CONSISTENT NAMING CONVENTIONS

Why It Matters

Power Apps encourages "under the hood" references to screens, controls, and variables. Having consistent naming for these items keeps your formula bar from turning into a puzzle.

Best Practices

1. **Prefix Controls**

   - For a text input on Screen1, name it "txtTitle" or "inp_Title." For a gallery, try "galTasks." This clarifies each control's purpose.

2. **Screen Naming**

   - Instead of "Screen1," call it "scr_Overview" or "scr_EditForm."

3. **Variable Consistency**

   - If you use variables (Set() or UpdateContext()), ensure they have descriptive names like varSelectedTask or locCurrentUserID.

Sarah's Realization

Initially, she left default names like "TextInput1" and "Screen2." As her app grew to five screens and 30+ controls, she lost track of references. A quick pass renaming them (e.g., "scr_MainGallery," "txt_SearchBox") made debugging and enhancements much simpler.

3. KEEP THE USER INTERFACE SIMPLE

Why It Matters

A busy, cluttered interface discourages users. They might be unsure which button to press or how to save changes. A clean, intuitive layout helps them complete tasks quickly and confidently.

Best Practices

1. **Limit Controls Per Screen**

    o   Too many text boxes and buttons can overwhelm. Use multiple screens if needed.

2. **Whitespace Is Your Friend**

    o   Add spacing around galleries, forms, and buttons. This approach prevents cramped visuals.

3. **Test on Mobile**

    o   If it's a phone layout, ensure tap targets are large enough and that labels remain legible on smaller screens.

Sarah's Insight

She initially stuffed her main screen with a gallery, three slicers, and a big form side by side. Colleagues found it confusing. Splitting into a "browse" screen and an "edit" screen improved clarity, letting them quickly see tasks or open the detail form only when needed.

4. USE FORMS AND GALLERIES WISELY

Why It Matters

Forms are great for editing single records, while galleries excel at listing multiple items. Mixing them effectively streamlines how users navigate and update data.

Best Practices

1. **Gallery for Browsing**

   o   Show a list of items. Let users tap one to view or edit details.

2. **Form for Editing**

   o   Separate screens or pop-ups with an Edit or Display form.

3. **Preview Carefully**

   o   Toggling between "DisplayMode = Edit" and "DisplayMode = View" can reduce confusion if you want a read-only vs. editable mode.

Sarah's Approach

She used a vertical gallery to list tasks and an edit form on another screen for in-depth changes. This separation avoided accidental edits while browsing. When a user wanted to update a task, a simple button triggered Navigate(scr_EditForm, None, {record: ThisItem}) so the form knew which record to load.

5. HANDLE NAVIGATION STRATEGICALLY

Why It Matters

In multi-screen apps, random or inconsistent navigation can leave users stuck or forced to guess how to return. A well-thought-out navigation flow fosters a natural user experience.

Best Practices

1. **Standard Button Placement**

o   Keep "Back" or "Home" icons in consistent spots (e.g., top-left corner).

2. **Use "Navigate()" Functions**

o   Keep transitions simple: Navigate(scr_Details, ScreenTransition.Fade).

3. **Breadcrumbs or Menu**

o   For larger apps, consider a simple menu bar or hamburger icon that reveals a screen list.

Sarah's Example

She placed a back arrow in the top-left corner of each detail screen, which used Navigate(scr_Main, None) to return. This predictable pattern helped teammates quickly learn the flow, even if they weren't tech-savvy.

6. THINK ABOUT PERFORMANCE AND LOAD TIMES

Why It Matters

As your app grows—especially if you connect multiple data sources—it can get sluggish. Users want apps that respond quickly, especially on mobile networks.

Best Practices

1. **Reduce OnStart Complexity**

o   If you load lots of data in App.OnStart, consider lazy loading (fetch data only when needed).

2. **Use Collect() or ClearCollect() Wisely**

o   Storing large tables in memory can slow the initial load. Load only key columns or filter data to essential rows.

3. **Optimize Data Calls**

o If you frequently read from the same data source, see if you can use cached local collections or create smaller sub-lists.

Sarah's Performance Tweak

She initially used OnStart to load entire SharePoint lists into collections. On slow connections, startup took 10 seconds. By collecting only the current user's tasks, load time dropped to under 2 seconds. The rest of the tasks loaded on demand when a user needed them.

7. EMBED SIMPLE LOGIC AND VALIDATIONS

Why It Matters

Ensuring clean data and preventing user errors can save you from headaches. A few well-placed formulas or conditions can ensure required fields, date checks, or consistent formats.

Best Practices

1. **Required Fields**

   o Mark important columns as required in your data source, or set Required = true in form controls.

2. **Conditional Warnings**

   o Use labels that appear only when certain conditions fail (e.g., If(txtEndDate < txtStartDate, true, false)).

3. **Regex or Filter**

   o For advanced scenarios, you can use IsMatch() for pattern matching, like email addresses or phone numbers.

Sarah's Example

Her team needed to ensure tasks had a due date after today. She set a condition so if a user tried to select a past date, a red warning label said "Due Date must be in the future," and the Save button was disabled. This tiny rule saved them from invalid data.

8. LEVERAGE ENVIRONMENTS AND ALMC

Why It Matters

In bigger organizations, having separate environments for development, testing, and production helps keep each stage stable and secure. Power Apps supports ALM (Application Lifecycle Management) if you want a more professional approach.

Best Practices

1. **Dev, Test, Prod**

   o Build and test new features in a Dev environment. Once stable, move them to Test for user acceptance, then push them to Prod.

2. **Solution Aware**

   o Wrap your app, flows, and other components in a **solution**. This simplifies moving the entire package between environments.

3. **Documentation**

   o Keep a short record of changes. If something breaks in production, you can trace it to a specific solution version.

Sarah's Organization

Initially, she used only the default environment. But as more teams built apps, IT set up a "DeptDev" environment for pilot versions. Sarah found that solution packaging made it easy to clone her app to new teams without messing up the original data source references.

9. EMBRACE POWER AUTOMATE AND POWER BI INTEGRATION

Why It Matters

Power Apps is part of a larger ecosystem. Tying in workflows from Power Automate or visuals from Power BI elevates your solution from a mere form to a robust platform.

Best Practices

1. **Trigger Flows**

   o A button in your app can run a Power Automate flow for approvals, alerts, or data updates in other systems.

2. **Embed Power BI Tiles**

   o Show real-time charts or key metrics from Power BI inside your app, guiding users with immediate insights.

3. **Look for Copilot**

   o AI features might help you design or debug your integrated flows. Don't shy away from letting Copilot propose solutions.

Sarah's Next Level

After building her task app, she embedded a small Power BI tile showing each user's weekly workload. This insight spurred better resource planning. She also added a "Send Alert" button that triggered a Power Automate flow whenever a high-priority task was created.

10. GET USER FEEDBACK AND ITERATE

Why It Matters

A Power App is rarely "done." If it solves a core problem, new ideas will naturally surface—improved fields, simpler screens, or expansions to new departments.

Best Practices

1. **Invite Early Feedback**

   o Don't wait for a perfect version. Share a prototype quickly, let your team test.

2. **Add a Feedback Screen**

   o Some creators add a quick form inside the app for
      suggestions. This fosters continuous improvement.

3. **Version Control**

   o Each time you make a significant update, note the
      changes. If something goes wrong, you can revert or
      debug systematically.

Sarah's Reflection

She initially built a "Task Form." After two weeks, her colleagues asked
for color-coded statuses, a due date filter, and additional fields for
"Complexity." She embraced these requests, refining the app. Iteration
turned a decent app into a beloved staple that truly matched the team's
needs.

Power Apps is all about fast, flexible, low-code development, but
longevity and adoption hinge on best practices—from neat naming
conventions and thoughtful UI design to performance optimizations and
feedback loops. As you follow these guidelines, your apps will remain
clear, efficient, and adaptable, even as your organization or data needs
grow.

Just like Sarah, you'll find that each improvement or new feature fosters
trust and excitement, building a culture where employees reach for
Power Apps whenever a manual or fragmented process slows them
down. In the next chapters, we'll move on to tips and tricks that can
elevate your app-building experience, show you how Copilot can
streamline development, and examine common pitfalls to dodge. Keep
refining, keep experimenting, and watch your Power Apps become
essential tools in your organization's daily workflow!

TIPS AND TRICKS FOR MICROSOFT POWER APPS

By now, you've learned how to craft a functional Power App: connecting data sources, building forms, and sharing the final product with your team. But once you start digging into the platform's deeper capabilities, you'll discover time-saving hacks, interface optimizations, and even AI-driven shortcuts that can make your apps sparkle. In this chapter, we'll explore a range of tips and tricks that can speed up development, enhance usability, and help you tackle trickier scenarios. Just like Sarah, who's continually refining her own solutions, you can take these suggestions to elevate your Power Apps projects beyond the basics.

1. MASTER THE FORMULA BAR

Why It's Helpful

Much like Excel, Power Apps uses an expression-based approach to control behaviors. A good understanding of the formula bar can save you from repetitive tasks and open up advanced logic.

Tricks

1. **Naming Consistency**
   - Reference controls by descriptive names (e.g., txtTaskName) in your formulas. This makes them more readable.

2. **Use "View → Data Sources"**
   - Quickly check which tables or connectors are being used in your formulas.

3. **Leverage IntelliSense**

o   As you type, Power Apps suggests functions and field
    names. Accepting these suggestions reduces typos.

Sarah's Shortcut

She found that pressing Alt while in the formula bar let her peek at
control references instantly. If a formula linked to "gal_Tasks," the alt-
based highlight indicated exactly which gallery or field was in use.

2. UTILIZE VARIABLES WISELY

Why It's Helpful

Local (UpdateContext) and global (Set) variables let you store values—
like user selections or filter criteria—without constantly querying data.
But overusing variables can lead to confusion if not managed carefully.

Tricks

1. **Local vs. Global**

   o   UpdateContext({varName: value}) for screen-specific
       states.

   o   Set(varName, value) for global states.

2. **Naming**

   o   Use a prefix (e.g., "loc_" or "var_") to distinguish local
       from global.

3. **Debugging**

   o   Check your variables under File → Variables to see
       current values or duplicates.

Sarah's Approach

She stored the currently selected task record in a global variable
Set(varSelectedTask, ThisItem) when tapping a gallery item. This made it
easy to reference the same record across multiple screens—like a detail
screen or confirmation dialog—without re-fetching from the data
source.

3. ADD CONFIRMATION POP-UPS OR TOAST MESSAGES

Why It's Helpful

When a user performs critical actions—deleting a record or submitting a complex form—it helps to provide a quick confirmation or success message. This fosters clarity and reduces accidental taps.

Tricks

1. **Use a Dialog Screen**

   o Hide or show it with a variable toggling visibility. A label might say, "Are you sure?" and buttons confirm or cancel.

2. **Notify Function**

   o Notify("Task saved successfully!", NotificationType.Success) can show a toast at the top of the app.

3. **Conditional Visibility**

   o You can set a container's Visible property to a condition, e.g., locShowDialog = true. A button toggles that variable.

Sarah's Polishing

She implemented a "Delete Task" button that triggered a small pop-up. If users clicked "Yes," it ran Remove(ProjectTasks, varSelectedTask). If "No," it closed the dialog. Her teammates appreciated the safety net, especially on mobile screens where taps are easily misplaced.

4. EXPLORE OFFLINE CAPABILITIES

Why It's Helpful

Field agents or remote employees might not always have reliable internet. Enabling offline means they can still capture data, and once connectivity is back, the app syncs updates automatically.

Tricks

1. **Use the LoadData() and SaveData() Functions**

   o   Save a collection locally on the device, then reload it when the app restarts.

2. **Check Connectivity**

   o   A label or icon might display If(Connection.Connected, "Online", "Offline").

3. **Sync Logic**

   o   When the device is online again, run a flow or a patch formula to upload offline records.

Sarah's Field Approach

Her team occasionally visited sites with no Wi-Fi. She built an "offline mode" that used local collections. A "Sync" button reconnected changes to SharePoint once they returned to coverage. This small addition turned a moderate app into a truly practical tool for on-the-go usage.

5. CUSTOMIZE THE THEME AND BRANDING

Why It's Helpful

A cohesive look and feel—fonts, colors, company logos—boosts professionalism and user trust. Consistency also helps different apps under your organization appear unified.

Tricks

1. **Use Themes**

   o   Under Home → Themes, pick a standard or create a custom theme in the advanced settings (using JSON for more fine-grained control).

2. **Design a Style Guide**

   o If your brand color is #0033AA, define it once in a style guide screen or variables. Then reference these variables in your controls' Fill or Color properties.

3. **Lockdown your layouts**

   o Use containers for a responsive design. This ensures elements scale nicely on different screens.

Sarah's Branding

She matched her app's accent color to her marketing team's logo, embedding a small banner at the top. This visual alignment made the app appear official, raising adoption rates. Her manager joked, "It looks like a real software product!"

6. USE REUSABLE COMPONENTS

Why It's Helpful

If you build multiple screens or multiple apps, certain controls—like headers, footers, or standard buttons—might repeat. Components let you design once and reuse them anywhere.

Tricks

1. **Create a Component**

   o In the left navigation, expand the Components area. Make a new one for a header bar with a logo and back button.

2. **Parameters**

   o Expose properties (like button text) so each instance can be slightly different.

3. **Import/Export**

   o You can move components between apps or share them with colleagues, ensuring a consistent user experience.

Sarah's Header

She built a reusable header with her team's logo on the left and a right-aligned "Log Out" icon. In each screen, she inserted this component instead of manually recreating the bar. If the logo needed to be updated, she changed it once in the component, and it propagated to all screens.

7. HARNESS AI CO-PILOT FOR QUICK BUILDS

Why It's Helpful

Copilot can turbocharge app creation or troubleshooting by suggesting entire screens, data connections, or formula improvements. If you're stuck or short on time, an AI prompt may yield a near-ready solution.

Tricks

1. **Describe Your Data**

   o In a canvas app, you might say, "Copilot, create a gallery that shows tasks, sorted by priority." The AI can scaffold that gallery.

2. **Refine**

   o If Copilot's output is slightly off, ask for adjustments: "Change the color scheme to match our brand" or "Use a vertical layout instead of horizontal."

3. **Debugging**

   o Stuck on a formula? Ask, "Copilot, why is my submit button not saving records?" The AI might spot an incorrect data source or a missing property.

Sarah's Speed Boost

While building a new "Client Feedback" screen, Sarah typed, "Copilot, design a form for collecting client satisfaction with rating and comments." Copilot generated a basic form with star rating controls. She tweaked the layout, but the heavy lifting was done automatically, saving her hours of trial and error.

8. MAKE DATA ENTRY EASIER WITH DYNAMIC CONTROLS

Why It's Helpful

If your app users do repetitive tasks—like selecting categories, statuses, or owners—let them search or pick from curated lists. Minimizing free-text fields reduces errors and speeds data entry.

Tricks

1. **Combobox vs. Dropdown**

    o   For large lists, a combobox with search built-in helps. For smaller sets, a simple dropdown might suffice.

2. **Auto-Filtering**

    o   If you have a field for "Assigned To," you can auto-filter names based on the user's department.

3. **Default Selections**

    o   Pre-fill a field with a common or recommended value: Default = "In Progress" for newly created tasks if that's typical.

Sarah's UI Refinement

She replaced a plain text input for "AssignedTo" with a combobox connected to her "UserDirectory" list. That way, coworkers simply typed the first few letters of a name to assign tasks. This cut down on misspellings and user frustration.

9. LEVERAGE POWER AUTOMATE FOR COMPLEX FLOWS

Why It's Helpful

Power Apps can manage data in real time, but sometimes you need heavier logic—like sending multi-step approvals, updating external CRM systems, or scheduling actions.

Tricks

1. **Add a Flow**

     o   In the top ribbon, select Action → Power Automate →
         "Create a new flow."

2. **Trigger from Buttons**

     o   A simple expression on a button's OnSelect could be
         MyFlow.Run(arguments...).

3. **Return Values**

     o   A flow can return output back into your app, letting you
         handle next steps accordingly.

Sarah's Automation

When a new high-priority task was submitted, she triggered a Power
Automate flow that emailed the manager, updated a "CriticalTasks"
SharePoint list, and posted a Teams alert in #urgent. The combined
synergy made the app feel far more robust than a simple form.

10. ASK FOR FEEDBACK, UPDATE, AND REPEAT

Why It's Helpful

No app is ever truly "done." As new processes emerge or user feedback
rolls in, iterating keeps the app fresh, relevant, and widely adopted.

Tricks

1. **Maintain Versions**

     o   Each time you publish changes, note them in a version
         log. If anything breaks, you can revert to a previous
         version.

2. **Encourage Suggestions**

o   In a stable environment, set up a "Phase 2 requests" channel or SharePoint site. Let users propose enhancements.

3. **Expand Your Data**

o   If usage grows, consider moving from Excel or SharePoint to Dataverse for more robust relationships and security.

Sarah's Cycle

She posted an internal poll asking "What's missing or confusing?" The replies suggested better search filters and color-coded statuses. After a short dev session, she republished with these changes. User satisfaction jumped, reaffirming that small tweaks can have a big impact.

Power Apps unlocks a new realm of rapid, user-friendly app creation, but mastering its nuances ensures your solutions shine. From naming conventions and offline design to advanced AI integrations and Power Automate flows, these tips help streamline both the building process and your final user experience.

Like Sarah, you can begin with modest forms, then grow your apps into sophisticated tools that unify data, optimize tasks, and spark a culture of innovation. In the upcoming chapters, we'll see how Copilot can further amplify your development speed, plus we'll walk through common pitfalls to watch out for. Keep experimenting, keep refining, and your Power Apps will elevate how your team works—one screen at a time!

YOUR AI-ENHANCED PARTNER IN POWER APPS

You've seen how Power Apps empowers anyone to build functional solutions without diving into heavy coding. But what if you could have a digital assistant by your side—someone to suggest screen layouts, write formulas, or point out data mismatches? That's the role of Copilot, Microsoft's AI helper in the Power Platform. By understanding natural language queries, Copilot guides you through tasks that might otherwise require trial-and-error or deep platform knowledge. In this chapter, we'll explore how Copilot can supercharge your app creation flow, troubleshoot tricky issues, and even propose design improvements. As you'll see with Sarah, adopting Copilot can shift you from "I wonder how to do that" to "Oh, Copilot just did it for me."

1. WHAT IS COPILOT IN POWER APPS?

AI-Powered Assistance

Copilot is an AI-based feature within the Power Platform that interacts with you much like a colleague who's knowledgeable about Power Apps design, data structures, and logic. Instead of searching endless documentation or trying random formulas, you can simply ask Copilot in natural language—like, "Help me create a form for my SharePoint tasks with a priority dropdown." Copilot then translates your request into actual elements (screens, controls, formulas) or step-by-step instructions.

Key Capabilities

- **Screen Generation**: Let Copilot scaffold entire screens—like a browse gallery, edit form, or data entry page—based on your data description.

- **Logic Suggestions**: Unsure how to patch records or filter galleries? Copilot can propose formula snippets or entire logic flows.

- **Troubleshooting**: Have an error in your app? Ask, "Copilot, why does my Submit button fail to save data?" It can analyze the formula or data connection and suggest fixes.

Sarah's First Encounter

When Sarah typed a basic prompt—"Copilot, create a list screen for my 'ProjectTasks' data source sorted by due date"—Copilot generated a vertical gallery connected to her list, automatically sorted by the 'DueDate' field. In mere seconds, she had a functional page, saving her from trial-and-error in the formula bar.

2. GETTING STARTED WITH COPILOT

Requirements and Availability

Copilot's features may require specific Microsoft 365 or Power Apps licensing tiers, so confirm with your admin or check Microsoft docs. You'll also want to ensure you're in a region and environment that supports Copilot previews or releases.

Activating Copilot

1. **Open the Maker Portal**: Go to make.powerapps.com.

2. **Check Settings**: Under Settings or Advanced Settings, look for toggles related to AI or Copilot.

3. **Look for Copilot Panel**: If enabled, you'll see a Copilot icon or sidebar. Clicking it opens a chat-like panel.

Once active, you can type queries or commands directly into the Copilot interface. It's best to start with small tasks—like adding a button or connecting a data source—then see how Copilot responds.

3. BUILDING SCREENS AND FORMS WITH AI

Natural Language Prompts

Instead of manually creating a gallery and hooking it to a data source, try describing your desired outcome:

- "Copilot, build a gallery to show open tasks from 'ProjectTasks,' sorted by priority."

- "Copilot, add a form for editing the selected task, and include fields: Title, DueDate, Status."

Copilot will propose an interface or a set of instructions. You can refine further: "Change the gallery layout to a horizontal list," or "Adjust the form to hide the 'Notes' field."

Instant Starter Apps

For brand-new solutions, you might say:

"Copilot, create a new canvas app connecting to my 'Requests' SharePoint list, with a main page listing requests and a detail page for editing them."
Copilot typically generates a multi-screen scaffold. While it may not be perfect, it saves you from repetitive steps—like setting Items, hooking up forms, or toggling display modes.

Sarah's Speed Boost

When a coworker asked for a quick "Expense Tracker," Sarah typed, *"Copilot, please create an expense tracking screen with fields for category, amount, and date, pulling from my 'Expenses' Excel file."* In less than a minute, Copilot had a workable screen. She tweaked the layout and theme, but the heavy lifting was done.

4. REFINING APP LOGIC AND EXPRESSIONS

Formula Guidance

Sometimes you know the outcome you want—like "Filter the gallery to show tasks due in the next 7 days"—but aren't sure of the exact formula. Copilot can propose something like:

Filter(ProjectTasks, DueDate <= (Today() + 7), Status <> "Completed")

You can then copy-paste or let Copilot insert it directly into the control's Items property.

OnSelect Actions

For button clicks or other triggers, you might ask, "Copilot, how do I patch a new record to my 'ProjectTasks' list with the fields Title, AssignedTo, and DueDate?" Copilot suggests the relevant Patch() expression, referencing your controls or variables. This approach can be a lifesaver for complex data operations, especially if you're not fully comfortable with the formula syntax.

Sarah's Logic

She wanted a button that assigned the currently viewed task to herself. She asked, "Copilot, show me how to set the 'AssignedTo' field of the selected record to the current user." The AI suggested a Patch formula that used User().Email as the new assigned value, and Sarah integrated it seamlessly.

5. TROUBLESHOOTING AND ERROR RESOLUTION

Diagnosing Issues

Copilot can help you pinpoint why a control or data connection isn't functioning as expected. For instance, "Copilot, why is my form not saving changes?" might yield a response noting that your form is still in read-only mode, or that you forgot to set the form's Data Source property.

Providing Alternative Solutions

If Copilot spots multiple possible issues—like a missing relationship or an incorrect formula—it can outline each possibility. This guided approach cuts down on guesswork or hours spent reading docs for a simple fix.

Sarah's Save Error

When her "Task Edit" form wouldn't update records, she typed, "Copilot, my Submit button doesn't work." The AI discovered that Sarah used SubmitForm(Form2), but the control was actually named Form_EditTask. Changing the reference resolved the issue instantly.

6. DESIGN ADVICE AND LAYOUT SUGGESTIONS

UI/UX Insights

Copilot might propose rearranging controls for clarity or adjusting color schemes to align with your brand. If you say, "Copilot, my screen is too busy—help me simplify," it could recommend splitting screens or grouping controls into a tabbed interface.

Responsive Tips

Creating a phone app that also looks okay on a tablet can be tricky. Ask, "Copilot, how do I enable responsive design?" It might show you how to use containers or dynamic sizing properties. While you might still need some manual tweaks, the AI guidance can set you on the right path faster.

Sarah's Layout Overhaul

She typed, "Copilot, I want a more modern design for my home screen—maybe a header with a welcome message and an icon for each main function." Copilot responded with steps to add an image control, a label, and some navigation icons. Sarah adapted the idea into a clean, tile-based layout.

7. EXPLORING ADVANCED CONNECTORS AND FLOWS

Linking to Third-Party Services

If you need to integrate a non-Microsoft data source, Copilot can suggest or set up connectors. "Copilot, connect this app to a Dropbox folder for attachments," might produce steps or partial code. You'll still authorize the connector, but the AI preloads relevant expressions.

Power Automate Integration

For advanced workflows—like emailing managers or updating on-prem systems—ask, "Copilot, create a flow to notify me when a new item is created in this app." The AI might suggest a template or guide you to the flow creation steps, bridging Power Apps and Power Automate seamlessly.

Sarah's Integration

She realized her marketing app needed to automatically send images to a cloud folder. She typed, "Copilot, upload any attached image to Dropbox when a user saves a record." Copilot explained how to add a Power Automate flow triggered by the app's OnSelect event, plus how to pass the image as a parameter. The final result removed manual steps for her marketing team.

8. ASKING FOR AI INSIGHTS OR FORECASTS

AI-Driven Data Analysis

While advanced analytics typically resides in Power BI, some limited AI can exist in Power Apps—like text analysis or sentiment detection. Copilot might show you how to call AI Builder models (like form processing or object detection) if you describe your scenario.

Future Plans

Microsoft continues to expand Copilot's ability to handle predictive tasks within the app itself. Keep an eye on updates; you might soon be able to do on-the-fly predictions or classification fully in your Power Apps environment.

Sarah's Experiment

After hearing about AI Builder, she said, "Copilot, can I automatically categorize tasks by complexity using AI?" The AI suggested linking an AI model that examined text fields and assigned complexity levels. Though it required an AI Builder license and some training data, the step-by-step guidance made it more approachable.

9. BEST PRACTICES FOR USING COPILOT

1. **Start Simple**

   o   Ask for one feature at a time. If you jump in with "Build a giant, multi-page app," Copilot might get confused.

2. **Verify and Refine**

   o   AI suggestions are not always perfect. Double-check formulas, test with sample data, and rename any auto-generated controls for clarity.

3. **Combine Human Creativity**

   o   Copilot might generate a layout that's functional but not exactly how you envisioned. Use it as a springboard, then manually tweak style, positioning, or advanced logic.

4. **Keep Learning**

   o   If you see Copilot produce a formula or approach that's new to you, read it carefully. Understanding the logic behind AI suggestions can expand your own skillset.

Sarah's Lesson

She quickly realized Copilot was best approached in iterative steps. She'd ask for a gallery, test it, then ask for a tweak, test again. She used what worked, ignoring or modifying suggestions that didn't quite fit. Over time, she built her own mental library of helpful patterns gleaned from Copilot's outputs.

10. LOOKING AHEAD

Copilot in Power Apps continues to evolve, promising deeper integration with data sources, more robust troubleshooting, and design recommendations that adapt to your usage patterns. By blending your domain expertise with AI's quick coding or formula suggestions, you can produce apps with remarkable speed and efficiency.

For Sarah, adopting Copilot has been a game-changer: tasks that once took hours of documentation-reading now get tackled in a single conversation with the AI. But she never treats Copilot as infallible—human validation remains key. As Microsoft refines the platform, you can expect more advanced prompts, better language understanding, and stronger synergy with other Power Platform tools.

With Copilot as a collaborator, you can go from "I have an idea for an app, but no clue how to build it" to "I deployed a working solution in less than a day." Embracing this AI-driven approach ensures your apps keep evolving in tandem with your organization's ever-changing needs. Next up, we'll explore common pitfalls in Power Apps—challenges even Copilot can't always avert without thoughtful planning. Stay tuned!

COMMON PITFALLS AND HOW TO AVOID THEM

Microsoft Power Apps can feel almost magical once you get the hang of designing screens and hooking into data. Yet, even with its low-code approach, there are still plenty of places you can stumble—whether it's performance woes, messy naming conventions, or overlooked security. In this chapter, we'll examine the most common pitfalls that can derail a promising Power App. By learning to spot these issues early, you'll deliver more polished solutions that make your users' lives easier. And as always, we'll see how Sarah navigated these challenges on her journey, turning near-disasters into valuable lessons.

1. MESSY DATA SOURCES AND STRUCTURES

The Pitfall

Starting your app with disorganized SharePoint lists, Excel sheets, or half-baked data leads to confusion and brittle formulas. Over time, adding or merging tables becomes a nightmare.

Why It Happens

Haste. You want a quick win, so you import an old spreadsheet or half-built list without tidying. Or you keep using multiple spreadsheets that evolve differently.

How to Avoid It

- **Standardize Your Data First**: Rename columns, ensure consistent data types, and remove unused fields before connecting to Power Apps.

- **Use the Right Tool**: For more complex relationships, consider Dataverse rather than layering multiple SharePoint lists.

- **Regular Cleanup**: Periodically revisit your data source to remove duplicates or test columns.

Sarah's Warning

She initially had a chaotic "ProjectTasks" sheet with unstructured text columns and some columns typed as numbers, others as text. In her app, certain fields wouldn't filter or sort correctly. After cleaning up the sheet—separating date columns from text fields—her formula errors vanished.

2. INCONSISTENT NAMING AND CONTROL MANAGEMENT

The Pitfall

Leaving default names like "Screen1" or "TextInput1" might seem harmless at first, but as your app grows, formulas reference a jungle of ambiguous objects.

Why It Happens

Early prototypes. You might say, "I'll rename things later," but you never do. Then your app hits 50 controls across 7 screens, and confusion reigns.

How to Avoid It

- **Adopt a Naming Convention**: e.g., scrMain, galTasks, frmTaskEdit, txtTitle, etc.

- **Rename As You Go**: Right after adding a control, rename it before building formulas.

- **Group Related Controls**: If your app is large, use the Tree View or containers to organize sets of controls.

Sarah's Lesson

Midway through building a 5-screen app, she faced a tangle of references. She paused, spent an hour renaming everything, and the clarity she gained saved her many headaches when changes needed to be made later.

3. UNMANAGED PERFORMANCE AND LOAD TIME

The Pitfall

Your app takes ages to load or becomes unresponsive, especially on mobile networks. Galleries lag, and users complain, "It's too slow to be useful."

Why It Happens

Unfiltered data calls, overly large images, or complex OnStart routines that fetch entire lists or multiple data sources at once.

How to Avoid It

- **Lazy Loading**: Only load core data in OnStart. Fetch additional data on-demand or when a user navigates to a specific screen.

- **Filter Early**: Instead of pulling thousands of rows into a local collection, filter them at the data source (e.g., "only tasks assigned to the current user").

- **Optimize Images**: Avoid embedding huge images in forms. Use attachments or references to smaller images.

Sarah's Improvement

She realized her OnStart was pulling entire lists for all users. She switched to filtering by User().Email so each user only got their relevant tasks. Load times plummeted from 10 seconds to 3, and her team stopped complaining.

4. CONFUSING USER INTERFACE AND NAVIGATION

The Pitfall

Users land on a cluttered main screen, can't figure out where to go, or how to get back after editing a record. They quickly abandon the app.

Why It Happens

You throw everything on one screen or lack a coherent flow. Each screen might have inconsistent button placements or unclear labels.

How to Avoid It

- **Plan the Flow**: Sketch how users will move (Home → Browse → Detail → Edit → Save → Back Home).

- **Consistent Navigation Icons**: Keep "Back" icons or "Edit" icons in standard locations.

- **Test on Real Devices**: Let a colleague try it on their phone. Watch where they get stuck.

Sarah's Redesign

Her first version jammed a gallery, a form, and multiple slicers together. After feedback, she split into distinct screens—"Task List" and "Task Details"—and added a clear "Back" button on the details screen. Colleagues immediately found the app more intuitive.

5. NEGLECTING SECURITY AND ACCESS CONTROLS

The Pitfall

Accidentally letting all staff see or edit confidential data. Or ignoring row-level restrictions, allowing managers to see tasks from other departments.

Why It Happens

Power Apps inherits a lot from underlying data sources. If your SharePoint or Dataverse permissions are too open, your app is too open. If you skip RLS, you can't limit data by user.

How to Avoid It

- **Check Data Source Security**: If using SharePoint, confirm list permissions. If using Dataverse, define appropriate roles.

- **Use Microsoft 365 Groups**: Restrict the entire app to certain user groups or individuals.

- **Row-Level Security**: For advanced control in Dataverse or model-driven apps, set up rules to filter records based on user roles.

Sarah's HR Glitch

She created a "Leave Request" app for her department but accidentally shared it with the entire company. Some staff saw internal requests they shouldn't have. She quickly fixed SharePoint list permissions and limited the app to the "HR Team" security group—lesson learned.

6. HARD-CODING VALUES INSTEAD OF USING DATA

The Pitfall

You embed user names, product lists, or environment URLs directly in your formulas. Any future change requires editing the app in multiple spots.

Why It Happens

You want a quick fix or don't see the need to store data externally. Over time, these "quick fixes" accumulate, complicating maintenance.

How to Avoid It

- **Use Data Sources for Lookups**: Even if it's a small table, keep it in SharePoint or Dataverse.

- **Leverage Variables**: If a value is used repeatedly, store it in a single variable or a parameter.

- **Environment Variables**: For environment or API URLs, store them in solution environment variables—making it easy to tweak in other environments without editing your app.

Sarah's Revelation

She'd typed "mgr@company.com" in multiple formulas for

notifications. When the manager changed, she had to hunt each formula. Switching to a "mgrEmail" field in her "AppSettings" list let her update it in one place whenever leadership changed.

7. FAILING TO HANDLE ERRORS OR VALIDATIONS

The Pitfall

Your app breaks if a user enters an invalid date or leaves a required field blank. Users might see a cryptic error or none at all.

Why It Happens

You assume minimal data checks, or rely solely on data source constraints. People skip needed fields or enter nonsense data.

How to Avoid It

- **Form Field Requirements**: Mark mandatory fields in the data source. Set "Required = true" in the form's properties.

- **Notify() on Errors**: If SubmitForm fails, show a toast message: If(Form1.Error <> "", Notify(Form1.Error, NotificationType.Error)).

- **Conditional Logic**: Disable the "Save" button if crucial fields are empty: DisplayMode = If(IsBlank(txtTitle.Text), Disabled, Edit).

Sarah's App Safeguards

Colleagues sometimes left "DueDate" blank, triggering weird date calculations. She set the form's DueDate field as required, displayed a label if it was missing, and blocked the Save button until it was filled. No more silent breaks.

8. OVER-RELIANCE ON A SINGLE SCREEN FOR ALL

The Pitfall

You try to handle everything—browse, detail, edit, advanced settings—on one canvas. It becomes unwieldy, with logic controlling when forms are hidden or shown.

Why It Happens

A desire for "simplicity" leads to bloat. Eventually, your single screen has complicated Visibility rules that confuse both builder and end users.

How to Avoid It

- **Multi-Screen Design**: Keep the main screen as a summary/browse, a second for detail/edit, maybe a third for advanced or admin functions.

- **Subscreens**: If you must keep it together, consider using hidden containers or tab-like navigation, but avoid overdoing it.

Sarah's Single-Screen Mistake

Her marketing requests app started as one screen with nested forms and pop-ups. She ended up with 20+ controls toggling visibility. Maintenance was a nightmare. Eventually, she broke it into a "Request Gallery," "Request Detail," and "Admin Settings" screen. The reorg improved performance and user clarity.

9. IGNORING ENVIRONMENT OR LIFECYCLE PRACTICES

The Pitfall

Everything sits in the default environment. Test apps, production apps, and random experiments all mingle, risking accidental changes or confusion about which version is "live."

Why It Happens

Early adopters might not realize how easily multiple environments can keep dev, test, and production separate.

How to Avoid It

- **Create Multiple Environments**: A dev environment for prototyping, a test environment for user acceptance, and a prod environment for final deployment.

- **Use Solutions**: Wrap your app and flows in solutions for better versioning and transport between environments.

Sarah's Organization

When the marketing team's test app accidentally replaced the live one, she learned about separate environments. They started using solutions to package the stable version, preventing unintentional overwrites.

10. NO ONGOING MAINTENANCE OR FEEDBACK LOOPS

The Pitfall

You build and publish a Power App, then never revisit it. Over time, data structures change, new fields are needed, or user requests go unaddressed—ultimately leaving the app to drift into irrelevance.

Why It Happens

You treat the app as a one-off project rather than a living solution that evolves.

How to Avoid It

- **Maintain a Backlog**: Encourage users to submit feature requests or bug reports.

- **Version Tracking**: Record changes in a simple doc or solution notes, so you can see how the app evolves.

- **Regular Check-Ins**: Schedule a brief review every few months to ensure the app's performance and relevance remain high.

Sarah's Continuous Improvement

Her HR leave request app started to lag behind new HR policies after six months. Users complained about missing fields. She realized a short quarterly meeting to review and update the app kept it fresh. Now it reflects the latest HR guidelines and remains popular.

Power Apps might be low-code, but it still calls for mindful design, data organization, and a willingness to adapt as needs grow. By learning from these common pitfalls—messy data, neglected performance, poor security, and more—you'll deliver an app that's not only functional but also a joy to use.

Sarah found that each "mistake" taught her how to handle data, performance, or user feedback more gracefully. The end result? Her department's apps run smoothly, new features roll out seamlessly, and colleagues trust the tool for daily tasks. With these pitfalls in mind, you'll be well-equipped to guide your own Power Apps journey—spotting early signs of trouble and steering each project to success.

Next up, we'll follow Sarah's comprehensive episode of building a real-world Power App from concept to deployment, reflecting how these best practices and tips shaped her final solution. Let's see how it all comes together in Sarah's full story!

SARAH'S APP ADVENTURE

The hum of her laptop fan was the only sound in Sarah's home office as she sipped her late-afternoon coffee, preparing to wrangle yet another spreadsheet. Her department had been tracking team requests in a shared Excel file—one that seemed to breed duplicates and conflicting updates every day. It had grown so messy that entire tasks vanished whenever two people edited the sheet simultaneously. "There must be a better way," Sarah thought.

Despite her success with automation through Power Automate and data insights with Power BI, building an app to unify her team's requests still felt like a leap. But that was before she'd taken a serious look at Power Apps—the low-code platform within the Microsoft 365 ecosystem. Little did she know she was about to kick off a project that would streamline her department's workflow.

Sarah's first big motivator came from a meltdown during a critical marketing campaign. Dozens of new content, design, and budget requests were piling up in their Excel file. Team members had no clear way to prioritize or see if another colleague was already handling a certain request. The chaos peaked when two managers accidentally overwrote each other's updates, losing half the tasks in the process.

"We can't keep losing data like this," Sarah's manager warned. "We need something more reliable." Memories of a short training session on Power Apps flashed through Sarah's mind. Could she build an app that captured requests in a structured form, assigned them automatically, and displayed them for everyone to see—without the risk of overwriting?

Idea: A simple "Request Tracker" app with a form for new requests, plus a gallery to see existing ones.

Sarah jotted down essentials for her minimal viable product (MVP):

- A "Requests" SharePoint list with columns for Title, RequestType, Priority, Owner, Status, and Notes.

67

- A Canvas App that displayed all requests in a gallery, and let users tap one to view or edit details.

- A quick link to notify the manager if a request was labeled "High Priority."

She decided on SharePoint because it was easy to set up and familiar to her team. More advanced solutions (like Dataverse) could come later if needed.

In the Power Apps Maker Portal, Sarah chose Create → Canvas app → Phone layout, naming it "RequestTrackerApp". She connected to her newly created Requests list. Instantly, a scaffold with a basic browse screen appeared, courtesy of the template wizard.

Her colleagues didn't quite realize how easy it could be. "Wait, you have a functioning list screen and detail screen already?" one coworker asked. "It only took a few clicks."

Sarah rearranged the default layout, adding her department's logo at the top. She renamed the auto-generated controls—"gal_Requests" for the main gallery, "btn_NewRequest" to add a fresh record. She placed a "+" icon in the top-right corner for new entries. For navigation, she used the built-in formula:

OnSelect = Navigate(scr_RequestForm, ScreenTransition.Fade)

This took users to the detail form screen.

When she struggled with a formula to filter requests by priority, Sarah typed into Copilot:
"Filter the gallery so it only shows requests marked 'High Priority.'"
Copilot proposed:

Items = Filter(Requests, Priority = "High")

She ended up adding a toggle so users could flip between "All Requests" and "High Priority." Copilot's suggestions became her personal coding mentor, saving hours of trial and error.

One of Sarah's biggest wins came when she realized she could embed a Power Automate flow directly from a button. For instance, the "Notify Manager" button ran a flow that emailed the manager with details of the request, plus posted a quick message in Teams—#urgent channel.

To set it up, she clicked Action → Power Automate in the ribbon, created a new flow named "NotifyManagerFlow," and had it accept parameters like RequestID, Title, and Priority. The flow used these parameters to craft a message. On the button's OnSelect, she wrote:

NotifyManagerFlow.Run(ThisItem.ID, ThisItem.Title, ThisItem.Priority)

After publishing, her manager praised the instant alert feature, saying, "I can act on these requests so much faster now!"

Colleagues often left out "DueDate" or assigned tasks to the wrong user. To reduce errors, Sarah set these fields as required in SharePoint and flagged them in the form. She added a rule: if IsBlank(DueDate), a label read "Due date is required" and the Submit button disabled. These small validations boosted user confidence.

At first, Sarah preloaded everything in App.OnStart—like user data, request categories, etc. The app took 8 seconds to start, which annoyed her coworkers. With Copilot's tip, she moved some queries to the relevant screens, so they only ran when needed. Load times improved drastically.

A near mishap happened when a coworker outside the marketing team stumbled upon the app and saw requests. Realizing the default environment allowed broad access, Sarah quickly restricted the SharePoint list to only marketing members. She also shared the app with that group specifically, thus preventing unauthorized eyes from seeing internal requests.

Soon, a traveling rep asked if they could submit requests offline. Sarah used Collect() to store new requests locally, then SaveData and LoadData to preserve them between sessions. The next time the user was online, a "Sync" button performed a Patch() to the SharePoint list.

This took a bit more logic, but it proved that even advanced scenarios were within reach.

The department recognized how polished the app could look. Sarah adopted a consistent color palette from the marketing brand guidelines—she even had Copilot suggest styling changes like a darker accent for the header. The final product felt official and coherent.

Sarah had only intended this for her own department, but word spread fast. Other teams were battling similar spreadsheet headaches, and they asked, "Could we get a version for our processes?" She realized how easily she could clone the app, tweak the data source or fields, and roll out a new solution.

"It's so simple to replicate," she marveled. "We're no longer waiting six months for IT to code a custom tool."

Setting Up a Dev-Test-Prod Flow

To maintain order, Sarah's IT mentor advised separate environments. She moved her original app into a "Test" environment for new features. Once stable, she used a solution to push updates to "Prod." This kept critical data safe and allowed for version testing. The added structure ensured no accidental overwrites or broken changes affected end-users.

Seeing the success, Sarah began brainstorming more advanced ideas:

- **Dataverse for Enhanced Relational Data**: If her department eventually needed more complex relationships—like multiple requests linking to clients and budgets—Dataverse might handle it better than a flat list.

- **Power Apps Portals** for External Requests: A public-facing form for external partners to submit collaboration proposals.

- **AI Builder**: Automate category assignment or sentiment analysis on request notes.

She also discovered that with a bit more coding, she could integrate external APIs to fetch up-to-date data from her CRM, blending external lead info into the app. "The best part is I'm no longer intimidated," she said. "I see how each new step builds on the fundamentals we've already mastered."

SARAH'S KEY TAKEAWAYS

1. **Data Prep Before App Prep**

   o Tidying her SharePoint list up front saved her from scattered expressions or complex patches later.

2. **Naming Conventions**

   o Renaming screens and controls from day one reduced confusion in formulas and references.

3. **Iterative Feedback**

   o Instead of launching a perfect app, she published a workable version quickly. User feedback shaped the final design.

4. **Copilot's AI Edge**

   o From hooking up flows to refining formulas, Copilot provided a second pair of eyes. She always validated its outputs, but it often sped up tasks she found tedious.

5. **Think Long-Term**

   o Setting up environment separation (dev/test/prod) and controlling app sharing prevented messy expansions and security slips.

Where once her team suffered from version-control chaos in Excel, Sarah's Power App introduced an organized, visually appealing solution that ran on phones and browsers alike. The shift also changed how her colleagues viewed technology: they became more open to self-service solutions. No longer did they assume "We have to wait for IT to build that." They started seeing problems as opportunities to innovate.

In short, "Power Apps turned me, a non-developer, into a solution architect," Sarah joked. But the results spoke for themselves: data was no longer lost, approvals sped up, and department morale improved—employees felt their voices were heard faster, leading to more efficient campaigns.

"It's not about fancy coding," Sarah reflected. "It's about giving teams the tools to craft their own solutions. That's the real power of Power Apps."

Sarah's experience stands as a testament: with a bit of courage, a willingness to learn, and some help from Copilot, building a custom app doesn't have to be a monumental effort. Every iteration brought new insights—whether it was best practices for data or tips from AI-driven suggestions. Her ultimate outcome was more than an app; it was a culture shift toward citizen development in her organization.

Your own journey might follow a similar arc. Start small, embrace feedback, and watch as your solutions become an integral part of your team's daily routine. With Power Apps by your side, you, too, can pioneer a transformation—one request form, one streamlined process, one new app at a time.

POWER APPS AND YOUR JOURNEY

From your first tentative steps—exploring data sources, dragging controls, and building forms—to crafting polished, responsive apps that solve real challenges, Microsoft Power Apps offers a remarkable journey. You don't need deep coding knowledge or an army of developers; with a bit of creativity and the right best practices, you can create functional solutions in weeks or even days. This book has shown how Power Apps can reshape your everyday processes and nurture a culture of innovation in your organization. Now it's time to step back, revisit the essential lessons, and reflect on how you can carry them forward—just as Sarah did when she realized the full potential of citizen development.

One of Power Apps' biggest strengths is its low-code approach, which lowers the barrier for non-developers. You learned how:

- Canvas Apps let you visually arrange controls, referencing data sources with formula-like expressions.

- Model-Driven Apps auto-generate interfaces from defined data models, perfect for more structured processes.

- Portals extend data access to external users, opening the door to customer or partner-facing solutions.

Even small, straightforward apps—like the ones Sarah built to manage tasks or marketing requests—can generate significant improvements, reducing reliance on scattered spreadsheets or overburdened IT teams.

From the earliest chapters, we stressed that clean, well-organized data is a prerequisite for effective Power Apps development. Ensuring consistent column names, proper field types, and minimal duplication across data sources (be it SharePoint, Excel, or Dataverse) saves you from convoluted logic and app performance issues down the line.

Whether you embed your app in Teams for quick collaboration, call a Power Automate flow from a button, or surface real-time analytics from

Power BI, the synergy of the Power Platform shines in Power Apps. By adopting these cross-app connections, you expand your solution's impact—transforming apps from stand-alone forms into holistic digital workflows that unify your data and tasks.

The book's middle chapters examined essential tips—from naming conventions and user-friendly interfaces to performance optimization and environment management. We also exposed common pitfalls like ignoring RLS, crowding a single screen, or skipping a feedback loop. Avoiding these obstacles helps keep your apps efficient, maintainable, and aligned with evolving business needs.

One of the newest boosts to Power Apps is the Copilot feature. By simply typing natural language requests—"Add a browse screen for tasks with priority filtering"—you can let AI draft essential components or fix errors in your formulas. This AI-driven approach accelerates development, enabling you to focus on fine-tuning design and logic. Sarah found that Copilot often tackled the drudgery, from writing patch formulas to spotting hidden references, allowing her to innovate faster.

Throughout the book, we followed Sarah, a resourceful team lead who discovered how a simple Power App could eliminate her department's spreadsheet chaos. Her progression highlights how citizen developers can confidently own their solutions:

1. **Pinpointing a Pain Point**

     o   An overcrowded, error-prone Excel file spurred Sarah to look for a better approach.

2. **Building the First MVP**

     o   By connecting to SharePoint data, Sarah rapidly created a Canvas App that listed tasks and forms, giving her team immediate relief.

3. **Refining with Feedback**

o   As teammates used the app, they requested features—filters, offline mode, and a button for quick notifications. She iterated to keep the solution relevant.

4. **Embracing AI Assistance**

o   Copilot handled formula suggestions, advanced integration tips, and design improvements, freeing Sarah to focus on strategic additions.

5. **Scaling Securely**

o   She learned about row-level security and environment separation, eventually rolling out the app across multiple teams. Her "dev-test-prod" approach safeguarded data and avoided overwriting the live app.

6. **Cultural Shift**

o   Ultimately, Sarah's story wasn't just about one app—it marked a shift in how her organization viewed digital innovation. She became a role model, proving that employees outside IT could tackle complex problems and implement robust solutions.

Microsoft regularly updates Power Apps with new connectors, UI elements, and AI features like Copilot enhancements. Stay curious—watch community forums, attend virtual sessions, and experiment with new functionalities. Each iteration might solve a challenge you've been grappling with or open a path to new use-cases.

The easiest way to adopt Power Apps is by addressing a modest, well-defined need—like a single data entry form or a process that's currently manual. Once colleagues see how quickly you can produce a working tool, they'll likely share more ideas or replicate your methods. Over time, small apps can evolve into bigger, more advanced solutions, possibly linking multiple teams or data sources.

Encourage peers to learn or at least observe Power Apps development. When employees across different roles brainstorm solutions, user requirements become clearer. Some may step up as co-owners of certain screens or logic, easing your maintenance load. It also ensures that your apps stay relevant, even if you move on or pivot to new projects.

If your organization embraces Power Apps broadly, define guidelines for environment usage, solution packaging, and data security—just like Sarah did. This avoids the "wild west" scenario where a hundred apps appear with varying quality and no central oversight. Good governance fosters creativity while keeping data secure and user experiences consistent.

The brilliance of Microsoft Power Apps is its capacity to let anyone become an app builder. You don't have to study computer science or wait months for a dev project to complete. By harnessing the platform's low-code interface, deep data connectors, and now AI-driven assistance, you can quickly address real-world pain points—be that simplifying an HR onboarding form, speeding up field inspections, or letting your sales reps update CRM data on the go.

Looking back at Sarah's adventure, a single question guided her transformation: "How can I solve this problem more effectively?" With Power Apps, she discovered the power of building her own solution, refining it based on user feedback, and ultimately championing a new way of working. Whether you're following in her footsteps as a first-time app creator or looking to expand an existing Power Apps ecosystem, the door is now open to a realm of limitless potential.

Remember: Start with data clarity, iterate with best practices, prevent pitfalls through mindful design, and let Copilot handle some of the heavy lifting along the way. By uniting business insight with Power Apps' low-code agility, you'll not only build functional tools but also shape a culture that thrives on citizen development and self-driven innovation.

As you close this chapter, keep these lessons alive in your future projects. Power Apps is ready whenever you face a new challenge. Let your ideas flourish, continue learning from your peers, and watch as each small app fosters a broader transformation in how your team or organization operates. You are now a part of the Power Apps story—just like Sarah— and the possibilities have only begun!

FROM LOW-CODE TO UNLIMITED POTENTIAL

As we conclude our exploration of Microsoft Power Apps, one central theme stands out: empowerment. By lowering the barriers to app creation, Power Apps enables everyone—from front-line employees to experienced IT pros—to solve problems, streamline processes, and share innovations across an organization. The result is more than just digitized forms or functional mobile screens; it's a shift in culture, where teams feel confident to shape their own solutions instead of waiting for external developers.

Throughout this book, you've learned how to:

- Select the right app type (Canvas, Model-Driven, or Portal) based on your data and user needs.

- Build and refine your app's design, connecting to data sources like SharePoint, Excel, or Dataverse.

- Adopt best practices for naming, performance, security, and user interface design.

- Leverage AI-powered Copilot to speed up formula writing, troubleshoot errors, and generate entire screens.

- Avoid common pitfalls like disorganized data, poor navigation, and lack of lifecycle governance.

- Iterate with feedback, ensuring your solution remains agile and relevant to evolving business scenarios.

Sarah's journey echoed each of these lessons, starting with a small app for her department but eventually influencing how her entire organization embraced citizen development. Her success story shows that a single, well-designed Power App can trigger a ripple effect—

boosting team morale, cutting down on manual overhead, and inspiring others to adopt the same approach.

Power Apps doesn't stand alone; it thrives in a larger ecosystem:

- **Teams**: Embed your apps in channels to keep data and conversations unified.

- **SharePoint**: Use Power Apps to replace or enhance SharePoint forms, bridging user-friendly interfaces with existing lists.

- **Power Automate**: Automate tasks triggered by app actions or data changes, creating an end-to-end workflow solution.

- **Power BI**: Embed real-time analytics or share data with your app, turning raw insights into actionable steps.

- **Copilot**: With AI-driven suggestions, you focus on creative logic rather than formula syntax.

As you integrate these tools, your apps grow from a single "departmental fix" into a robust, enterprise-ready platform that can scale, adapt, and deliver continuous value.

If your apps outgrow basic lists or spreadsheets, consider Dataverse for more complex relationships, enhanced security, and advanced business logic. Over time, you might also explore Model-Driven Apps or Power Apps Portals to engage external audiences.

As more teams adopt Power Apps, establishing clear environment and solution management helps maintain order. Encourage developers and citizen creators to adopt version control, separate dev/test/prod environments, and adhere to naming and security standards.

Stay informed on new Copilot capabilities or AI Builder improvements that can further streamline tasks like data categorization, sentiment analysis, or advanced forms processing. The platform evolves constantly—regular check-ins on Microsoft's updates can spark fresh ideas.

The Power Apps community is thriving, with forums, blogs, and user groups sharing tips and templates. Engaging with peers not only sharpens your skills but also keeps your solutions aligned with best practices. If you're comfortable, share your own success stories or app templates to help others.

Ultimately, Power Apps is about more than building a single tool; it's about rethinking how your organization solves everyday problems. Traditional app development requires specialized resources, lengthy timelines, and sometimes big budgets. Power Apps flips that script, letting real-world domain experts—like Sarah—craft solutions precisely tailored to their needs. This citizen development approach unlocks creativity, agility, and a sense of ownership among team members, fostering a culture where innovation is everyone's responsibility.

"We used to say we can't do that until IT frees up," Sarah often recounts, "but now we say let's prototype in Power Apps first." It's a subtle yet powerful shift that can transform how your company tackles challenges.

Thank you for joining us on this Power Apps journey. Whether you're a seasoned Microsoft 365 user or just dipping your toes into low-code, you now hold the keys to building fast, impactful solutions that can grow with your imagination. Remember:

- Start small with one pain point—like a paper form or scattered data.

- Iterate quickly, gathering user feedback to refine.

- Adopt best practices for data structure, naming, and security.

- Lean on Copilot or the community when you hit roadblocks.

- Share your success, inspiring colleagues to experiment and adopt a citizen developer mindset.

As you continue exploring the platform, keep an eye out for new connectors, AI features, and integration opportunities that can push your solutions further. Power Apps is only one piece of the broader Microsoft 365 puzzle; combined with Teams, SharePoint, Power Automate, and more, you can unify digital workflows across your entire organization.

From paper-based chaos to dynamic, interactive apps—Power Apps is your catalyst for turning vision into reality. Let your ideas flourish, your creativity shine, and your enterprise benefit from solutions built by the people who know its needs best: *you* and your fellow citizen developers. Go forth and create, innovate, and transform—one Power App at a time!